Praise for *Walking with Go*

MW00576518

"Navigating life is what becomes a challenge for all of us! What is so refreshing about Fr. Mike's book, *Walking with God in the Unimpressive Seasons of Life*, is that it's doable, but only doable by sharing the burden and challenges with God. He encourages us to meet the challenges, approaching them like a book, one page at a time. If you keep reading, you will finish the story, and isn't that what life is anyway, a story? Or as Pope St. John Paul II said, 'a pilgrimage to our Father's house'? Sure, the single pages of our life might be unimpressive, but when you put them all together, it's one impressive story. Don't write your whole story in one day. Relax and take Fr. Mike's advice when it comes to 'walking with God'! Before you know it, you'll be standing before God!"

—Jeff Cavins, creator of *The Great Adventure* Bible studies, podcaster, and pilgrimage host

"Thanks be to God for Fr. Mike! With his typical engaging and encouraging style, he helps us to see that real change in life often happens in small moments rather than big, dramatic ones. We can make big strides in personal holiness, one small step at a time."

—Danielle Bean, writer, speaker, and host of the *Girlfriends* podcast

"As you might guess, as a Franciscan priest, I love St. Francis. One of the attributes that I love about St. Francis is that he had the ability to see God in the ordinary things and moments of life. Whether it be a sunrise, a gentle rain, a leper, or a sinful priest, Francis was able to see God in all things. This is what I appreciate about Fr. Mike's book, *Walking with God in the Unimpressive Seasons of Life*. With simple wisdom, Fr. Mike helps the reader discover God in the ordinary journey of life. By using examples of people we know, like biblical figures and saints, or more obscure athletes, the reader discovers that finding God in the ordinary changes how we see God and how we see ourselves. This is central to the life of the saints and hopefully the fruit of Fr. Mike's book."

—Fr. Dave Pivonka, TOR, president of Franciscan University of Steubenville and founder of wildgoose.tv

"Don't underestimate yourself or the power of this little book—it could be the most important work you will ever read outside of the Bible. Fr. Mike Schmitz explains how the single unifying principle of loving Jesus and making him known changed ordinary people into extraordinary saints and how by following this same principle your life, and mine, can be similarly used by God. Fr. Mike walks us through how this is accomplished—it is not complicated or overwhelming; it is quite simple really. It is achieved one moment at a time and by one small choice at a time. If you want your life to be forever changed, discovering how to have a God centered focus and mission, come along on this expedition. You will never regret one single step you take that leads you closer to God and his great purpose for your life. Fr. Mike is the perfect companion for your journey."

—**Melissa Overmyer**, founder of Something Greater Ministries and author of *Wisdom from Women in Scripture*

FR. MIKE SCHMITZ

WALKING
WITH GOD
in the
unimpressive
SEASONS
of LIFE

Published by The Word Among Us Press

7115 Guilford Drive, Suite 100,

Frederick, Maryland 21704

wau.org

28 27 26 25 24   1 2 3 4 5

ISBN: 978-1-59325-722-4

eISBN: 978-1-59325-723-1

Design by Rose Audette

Library of Congress Control Number: 2024904534

Contents

ONE SMALL STEP

Don't Underestimate Your Role in God's Plan

D id you know that only 8 percent of people who have set New Year's resolutions actually accomplish them? In fact, the majority of people give up by January 12! We quit in under two weeks! Maybe you are a New Year's resolution person. Maybe you're a student and you've told yourself: *This semester, I'm going to live at the library.* Or maybe you've decided that this year, every day at 6 a.m., you're going to work out. Or this year, you're going to be all about relationships and not as focused on work.

What happens when we make New Year's resolutions is not that we overestimate our goals or dreams—the big moments and the big plan. It's that we underestimate the impact that our daily choices and small decisions can have. When it comes to any change we desire in our lives, *we underestimate what God sees in us.* We underestimate the power of the single, unifying

Too often, we
underestimate
ourselves and what
God wants to do
with us.

principle for our lives. Too often, we underestimate the impact of those small daily decisions. Too often, we underestimate ourselves and what God wants to do with us.

In this book, we will be looking at how, too often, we underestimate who God sees us to be, what God wants us to be, and what God can do in our lives. We will ask: *Where am I underestimating myself? And how am I underestimating God's power in my life?*

The Power of a Single Unifying Principle

A few years ago, I read an article about the Olympic British Cycling Team.[1] This team was awful! For more than 110 years, no cyclist in Great Britain had won the Tour de France. One of the top European bike manufacturers wouldn't let them use their bikes because they were too embarrassed to be associated with them. Had you been around, you would have estimated that they were not good; they were mediocre at best!

But then in 2003, the team hired a new trainer named Dave Brailsford. Everyone had estimated this team as being bad at competitive cycling, but Brailsford saw this team and refused to underestimate them. He believed they had the potential to be amazing—to be far more than what everyone assumed them to be. So he told them, "Because you have the potential to be more, you *need* to be more."

I think God wants to say something similar to us. In Isaiah 49, God speaks to the Israelites in the Northern Kingdom. God

---

1 See James Clear, *Atomic Habits* (New York: Penguin Random House, 2018), 13–15.

I believe that many of us have underestimated our role in God's story, and because of that, we have underestimated who God needs us to be.

had promised that David's kingdom would last forever. But after King Solomon's reign, the kingdom of Israel split into ten tribes in the North and two tribes in the South. Then the Assyrians came and destroyed the ten northern tribes. But along comes Isaiah to tell the remnants of this Northern Kingdom that they will restore Israel. He tells them, essentially, "You are mine. You're my servant. You are going to restore those tribes. You're going to restore Jacob" (see 49:1-5). Then he goes even further: "It is too little . . . for you . . . to raise up the tribes of Jacob / and restore the survivors of Israel; / I will make you a light to the nations, / that my salvation may reach to the ends of the earth" (49:6). He is saying, "I've called you to this impossible task. But this bar is actually too little! You will not merely restore the kingdom; you are going to do more. You are going to be a light to the nations." Here's the thing: when you underestimate your role in God's plan, you underestimate who God needs you to be. God tells the Israelites, and he tells us, that *they have underestimated what God can do in them and through them.*

This is our story. I believe that many of us have underestimated our role in God's story, and because of that, we have underestimated who God needs us to be. Because if you have a great role, that means you have to be a great person.

Now, some of you might think, "Wait, I'm already overwhelmed, and now you're telling me that I'm not even where I need to be? That I need to be more?" We can be so exhausted trying to be perfect in everything, juggling so many roles that we need to play. We feel we have to be a good son or daughter. We have to be a good brother or sister. We have to be a good disciple of Jesus, a good spouse, a good employer or employee, a good roommate, a good friend. And we end up feeling so torn

What if we established
a single unifying principle
that could knit together
all those separate threads
that seem to be tearing
us apart, to make one
beautiful image?

and worn out, pulled in too many directions of ideals we need to live up to. In this way, we can find ourselves with a divided heart and a divided life. It can be exhausting. Even Sunday Mass and daily prayer can feel like a burden and just one more direction we're being pulled in.

But what if we realized the power of our role? What if we no longer underestimated who God wants us to be? What if we established *a single unifying principle* that could knit together all those separate threads that seem to be tearing us apart, to make one beautiful image?

One Moment at a Time

John the Baptist is an excellent example of someone who lived by a single unifying principle. God had called him to be the greatest prophet of all time, and that's a lot to live up to! So how did he fulfill his calling and not get torn apart by the demands of that incredible role? Listen to what he says.

"The reason why I came baptizing with water was that [Jesus] might be made known to Israel" (John 1:31). There's a lot in this one sentence. It's as if John is saying, "The reason why my parents couldn't have a child until they were both old, the reason why an angel appeared to my father in the Temple, the reason why I was consecrated from the womb, why I have not drunk any wine, why I've lived in the desert my entire life, the reason why I eat nothing but honey and grasshoppers and dress in camel's hair, and the reason why I baptize—it's all so that Jesus might be made known. Everything that has happened in my life is united by this one single principle: that Jesus can be known."

Saints are just people
who didn't underestimate
who God needed them
to be.

What was John's guiding principle? Why did he do anything he did his entire life? For that one reason: so that he would know Jesus, and so that Jesus would be made known. He wasn't perfect. John didn't know Jesus. He didn't know his own cousin. Because when he was weaned, he was sent to the desert, to live with a community, the Essenes. John was separated from his entire family. But he knew the single unifying principle of his life was: *Someday I'm going to know him, and someday I'm going to make him known.*

The same goes for us. You might not know everything that God wants you to do, but if you live according to the single unifying principle of knowing Jesus and making him known, there is no way you can fail to become the kind of person God wants you to be. We cannot underestimate the power of this single unifying principle.

John gave his whole life for this. So how did he do it? One moment at a time. One choice at a time. It wasn't in the big things or the big moments; it was in the small moments. Think about any loving couple you know. They give their whole lives to each other, and they do it one moment at a time. One choice at a time. Think of any person who has ever done something incredible. How did they give their whole life to that passion or that project? They did it one moment at a time. One choice at a time.

What's in Front of You?

Saints aren't made in big moments. Saints are just people who didn't underestimate who God needed them to be. They didn't underestimate the power of a single unifying principle. They

St. Francis of Assisi realized God was calling him to bring renewal to the whole Church. And he began by doing the small thing right in front of him.

refused to underestimate the impact of small decisions. Instead they just did what was in front of them.

We all know St. Francis of Assisi. When he was about twenty years old, he had a conversion, and then everything in his life was knitted together by the single unifying principle of knowing Jesus and making him known. But he didn't know what to do.

One day as he was praying in front of a crucifix, the crucifix spoke to him. The image of Jesus on the cross said, "Francis, rebuild my Church, for it is falling into ruin." The Catholic Church at that time was experiencing a lot of corruption, but St. Francis didn't go immediately to Rome and say, "I'm here to fix things." He looked around and saw that the chapel he was praying in was falling apart. So he put one stone on top of another and literally rebuilt the chapel. It was only over time that he realized God was calling him to bring renewal to the whole Church. And he began by doing the small thing right in front of him.

The Power of Small Changes

Dave Brailsford, the coach for the British cycling team, refused to underestimate the power of small things. When he became the coach in 2003, he had a single unifying principle: to become the best cycling team in the world. He didn't fire the team and get all new athletes. He just took those mediocre athletes and made them into great athletes. How? By aiming to be 1 percent better every day.

The team started with the obvious things. They adjusted the height and angle of their bicycle seats so that they could get the maximum power output. They started wearing heated shorts

What would a 1 percent
change look like in
your life?

to keep their muscles at the proper temperature. They used wind tunnels and experimented with different fabrics. They researched which massage gels actually helped recovery after practices. They brought in a doctor to teach them the best way to wash their hands to prevent illness. They experimented with different kinds of pillows for each cyclist to find which pillow maximized the rest he got. They painted the inside of the team van white so that they could spot any dirt that might get into the bicycle gears. Coach Brailsford did not underestimate the power of those small decisions.

Five years later, they competed in the 2008 Beijing Olympics, and they won 60 percent of the gold medals in cycling. Four years later in London, they set nine new Olympic records and seven world records. They hadn't won the Tour de France in 110 years. In 2012, they won. And again in 2013 and 2015, 2016, and 2017. Between 2007 and 2017, they won 178 World Championships and 66 Olympic and Paralympic gold medals.

This is the power of small changes—the aggregation of marginal gains that other people underestimate.

A 1 Percent Change

You can't underestimate who God needs you to be. You can't underestimate the power of that single unifying principle. *God needs you to know Jesus and to make him known.* So don't underestimate small changes.

What would a 1 percent change look like in your life? Something simple. For example, athletes set out their clothes before going to bed so that they're ready to work out when they

We cannot underestimate the power of small steps because that's what made Olympians out of mediocre athletes.

wake up. If your unifying principle is to know Jesus and make him known, maybe you could make sure you get to bed on time so that you can wake up on time. Maybe you could set out your Bible and your prayer journal at night so that they're there, ready for you when you wake up.

Athletes don't decide what they're going to do when they go to the gym. They decide what they're going to do *before* they go to the gym. What about us? If my single unifying principle is to know Jesus, what kind of way can I pray to make sure that I'm going to know him? Like some smartwatches today that remind us to stand up every hour, maybe every time your watch strikes a new hour, you could pull out a Scripture verse to reflect on or keep a copy of a missalette to help you reflect on the Mass readings.

Refuse to Underestimate

I was in an airport not too long ago, and I wasn't wearing my clerics. I was working on my computer, and on the back of the computer I had a sticker that said, "Seen, Known, and Loved." A soldier sitting next to me saw the sticker and asked me, "What's that about?" So for the next twenty minutes, I got to talk to him about what I do and the fact that God has a plan for his life.

We cannot underestimate the power of small steps because that's what made Olympians out of mediocre athletes. It's what has made saints out of ordinary people. If God has done that with mediocre athletes and ordinary people, imagine what God can make out of you if you refuse to underestimate what he can do!

SILENCE IS NOT ABSENCE
Don't Underestimate the Value of Time

On college campuses, the spring semester is all about spring projects: getting portfolios together, theater productions, thesis papers, etc. The question is: with a big project ahead of you, how long do you think it will take you to get that project done?

In 1977, two psychologists, Daniel Kahneman and Amos Tversky, conducted a study to prove how easy it can be to underestimate how much time it will take to accomplish a task.[1] They called it the "planning fallacy." In this study, they found that humans have a tendency to disregard historical data when it comes to making predictions. Even though we may have done the same project before and it took us a certain amount of time, we think it will take us less time the next time we do it. In fact, we think it will take us half the time it will actually take.

---

1 Roger Buehler, Dale Griffin, and Michael Ross, "Exploring the 'Planning Fallacy': Why People Underestimate Their Task Completion Times," *Journal of Personality and Social Psychology* 67, no. 3 (1994): 366–381.

If becoming who God needs us to be is the project of our lives, we have to be prepared to actually let it take our entire lives.

Another study in 1997 observed thirty-seven psychology seniors writing their senior theses. The researchers asked the students to estimate how long it would take them to write their senior thesis. The average estimate was thirty-four days. The best case was twenty-seven days. In reality, the average amount of time it took them was fifty-five days; that's three weeks longer than they initially thought! And this, even though they had written many papers before.

A few years later, a woman was writing an article about this planning fallacy, and she discovered that she too was guilty of it.[2] She tells how she painted five rooms in her house. When she began with the first room, she thought, "It'll take me a weekend. It's not a big room." But it took her a month. So when she went to paint the second room, she said, "Okay, I know the last room took me a month, but now that I've done it once, this room should take me only a weekend." It also took her a month. So the third time she said, "Okay, I'm not going to be fooled this time. Now that I really know how to do this, I'm sure it will take me only one weekend." Again, it took her a month. The same thing happened for each of the five rooms she painted. She says that if she ever paints a sixth room, she won't disregard her historical data, no matter what she thinks!

The Project of a Lifetime

In the last chapter, we talked about how we cannot underestimate who God needs us to be. In this chapter, I want to talk

---

2 Jessica Greene, "Why We're Bad at Estimating Time (and What to Do about It)," February 25, 2019, Zapier, https://zapier.com/blog/how-to-estimate-time/.

In relationships, there
are some things that only
time can reveal.

about how we cannot underestimate how long it will take to become who God needs us to be. If this is the project of our lives, we have to be prepared to actually let it take our entire lives.

So what kind of people does God need us to be? He needs us to be the kind of people who love heroically. He needs us to be the kind of people who can trust heroically. And love and trust are two things that have to grow. I wish you could just wave a wand over someone and make them more trusting or make them love deeply. But you can't. Because growth takes time. No matter how badly we want it to be done right away, it takes time. In order for our love to be powerful and our trust to be deep, it has to grow; it has to take time.

I once had a couple ask me to preside over their wedding on the one-year anniversary of the day they started dating. They had been dating for about four months at that time, and they told me, "Father, we know we were meant to be married." "But you have to have the big conversations," I told them. They said, "We've already had the big conversations. What do you think we were doing the first four months of our relationship?" I had to tell them "No" in the kindest, gentlest way. We negotiated their wedding date because the reality is that you can have those big conversations from the very beginning, but in relationships, *there are some things that only time can reveal.*

Another couple who had been dating for two and a half years met with me two months before their wedding. They said, "Father, we have to let you know that you're right." "About what?" I asked. "You told us that the feeling of being in love was going to pass. We thought that it wouldn't happen to us, but two months ago, it happened. Now, we're free. We're free to walk away from each other, but we're also free to get married

We can't underestimate
how important and
necessary even the
lowest times in our
lives are.

to each other." This—losing the feeling of being in love—is not a bad thing. It's actually very necessary. And we can't underestimate how important and necessary even the lowest times in our lives are.

Times of Darkness and Silence

The Bible is full of stories of people who had to wait—who, in spite of walking in faith, found themselves walking in darkness. They were desperate for God, crying out to him. The Israelites, once part of a kingdom made up of twelve tribes, found themselves obliterated by the Assyrians. The two tribes first destroyed were Zebulun and Naphtali. Keep in mind that God had promised that his kingdom would last forever. The Israelites absolutely felt like God had abandoned them, like God wasn't doing anything in their lives. This low point lasted so long!

Have you ever had this experience? Where you decided to take a step of faith, and then, nothing? And sometimes, worse than nothing. But you keep on trying, praying—all the while walking in darkness.

Another person in the Bible who experienced this kind of waiting through tough times is Daniel. In Daniel, chapter 10, he tells of a vision he had in which he saw this massive war where there was so much destruction and death that he felt as if he might die just looking at it. Afterward, he says, he mourned for three full weeks: "I ate no savory food, took no meat or wine, and did not anoint myself at all until the end of the three weeks" (10:3). During this whole time, Daniel prayed and begged God to show him what the vision meant. But God seemed to be silent.

God's silence is not
the same thing as
his absence.

Have you ever felt that way?

But then on the twenty-fourth day, Daniel looked up and saw an angel, who told him what the vision meant. Daniel fell unconscious, but the angel said, "Do not fear" (10:12). And he gave this answer: "From the first day you made up your mind to acquire understanding and humble yourself before God, your prayer was heard. Because of it I started out, but the prince of the kingdom of Persia stood in my way for twenty-one days, until finally Michael, one of the chief princes, came to help me" (10:12-13).

From the moment Daniel started to pray, God heard him. But he didn't know. You see, God already knew Daniel's need, but Daniel didn't know that. He had to wait for God to answer, and there were times it felt as if no answer would come. But the truth is, we cannot underestimate what God is doing when it seems that God is doing nothing—because his silence is not the same thing as his absence. *Sometimes, in fact, his silence is absolutely necessary.*

God's hiddenness is not the same thing as his inactivity. Something is happening in this silence, in this darkness, even in this brokenness. You may not know the next steps; you may not know what God wants from this, what God is doing. But we cannot underestimate what God is doing in this. The truth is that something is happening that is absolutely necessary.

If you've ever tried to grow Chinese bamboo, you can get a sense of what I mean. You plant the seed and you water it and make sure it has everything it needs. Nothing happens for the first year, so you keep taking care of the soil. Nothing happens the second or the third or the fourth year. Actually, something is happening, but you just can't see it. For those four years, that

While we're waiting, God is doing something in the silence that he couldn't do without that silence.

Silence Is Not Absence: Don't Underestimate the Value of Time

seed has been setting out a root system that goes so wide and goes so deep underground that when the fifth year comes, that bamboo seed sprouts and grows up to ninety feet in five weeks. When it seemed like that seed was doing nothing, something necessary was happening. Without that breadth and foundation, the bamboo tree could not be supported.

The same is true for us. While we're waiting, God is doing something in the silence that he couldn't do without that silence. He is doing something in our brokenness that he couldn't do without that brokenness.

He is doing something in the darkness that he couldn't do without that darkness. He is making us into people who can trust. You can't trust unless you need to trust, and that's how he uses the times of darkness and silence and brokenness.

Turn the Page

But what should we do in those times when we're waiting and God seems to be doing nothing? *Turn the page.* Have you ever been reading a book, and you get to a part where something really bad happens to your favorite character, and you just stop reading and throw it against the wall? But then you pick it up again, and you keep reading because you want to know what comes next. Just because something terrible has happened doesn't mean you abandon the story. It means you turn the page.

The last book of the Old Testament is the Book of the prophet Malachi. If you were to stop reading the Bible at the end of Malachi, you'd probably be pretty disappointed. You'd wonder what happened to all the things God had promised he would

To live in this world of
uncertainty is to walk
in darkness.

do. But if you just turned the page—just one single page—you would come to the Gospel of Matthew and the story of God fulfilling all these promises. There is one page between Malachi and Matthew, from the prophet Malachi to John the Baptist. That one page represents four hundred years.

It's the same for us. We find ourselves in this darkness, in a terrible part of the story—maybe in a terrible season of the story. What does God say? *Turn the page.*

There's a passage in the Book of Isaiah that says, "The people who walked in darkness / have seen a great light" (9:1). The people weren't just standing in the darkness; they were *walking* through it. That's what it is to live, my friends: to live in this world of uncertainty is to walk in darkness.

The philosopher Søren Kierkegaard said something similar when he said that life can only be understood backward, but it must be lived forward. We can truly understand our life only when we've already lived through it and look back to see everything that has happened over all those years. Until then, we have to live it forward. We have to keep walking. We have to finish the story because there's no way to know how the story is going to end until the story has actually ended. In the meantime, you do what you know to do: you remember; you keep walking.

In the End . . .

We can learn a lot from the story of Gideon. We read about him in Judges. The people of Israel were being terrorized by the Midianites. They were so small and poor, and the Midianites were terrorists. They violently attacked the Israelites, and

We just have to keep reading, to turn the page and finish the story.

they also did psychological warfare. They would poison their wells, kill their animals, and wait until the Israelites planted their crops to destroy them.

At one point, an angel appears to Gideon. "The LORD is with you, you mighty warrior!" he says (Judges 6:12). Gideon responds, "If the LORD is with us, why has all this happened to us? Where are his wondrous deeds? . . . For now the LORD has abandoned us and has delivered us into the power of Midian" (6:13). The angel answers him, and I paraphrase, "The Lord has heard you, he's answered you. He's with you in your woundedness, brokenness. He's going to fight for you."

Gideon tells the people about this message and thousands of people show up to fight. But God says, essentially, "I don't want to win with thousands of people, because you're going to think you did it." So they whittle down. They surround the camp of Midian with swords and trumpets. They break their cover and blow the trumpets, shouting, "For the LORD and for Gideon!" (Judges 7:18). The Midianites then wake up and kill each other.

I was recently talking to a missionary at the campus where I work. She was talking to a student who said that she had encountered Jesus in an entirely new way when she got to campus. The student said, "Do you ever have the experience of going into the chapel and you can't stop crying because of how much Jesus loves you?" The missionary replied, "No, I don't. I wish I did." But that was her experience. She would weep. This year, the same student says she can't even pray. She shows up and it feels like God isn't even here. She says, "I actually forget what it was like when I would weep before Jesus."

That's us too. In the darkness, we forget what was true in the light. We think God's not doing anything. But he's there.

In the darkness,
we forget what was
true in the light.
We think God's not
doing anything. But
here's there.

We just have to keep reading, to turn the page and finish the story. Because there's no way to know how the story is going to end until it's actually ended. Then we'll know. Then we'll understand. But until then, we cannot underestimate what we don't understand.

In the end, God restored the Israelites. In the end, he lifted them up. In the end, he transformed all of that pain. The people that were once decimated were lifted up and transformed. It didn't happen immediately after their kingdom was obliterated by the Assyrians. It happened years and years later, when Jesus came to live in it.

God Will Use It All

So are you okay with temporary suffering? With enduring a time of suffering, knowing that God will restore you in the end? Are you okay with temporary loss if, in the end, God will use it all? Are you okay with temporary pain if, in the end, it all matters? Because that's what he promises.

When we come before God, we pray for healing, for reconciliation, for a future . . . and God can do all those things. We also know that healing and reconciliation and recovery are not the only possible outcomes when we are suffering. Death is also a possible outcome. Not finding a spouse is a possible outcome. Lifelong illness is a very real possibility. But God is still present in those things. He is still active even when my chapter is over. The story still goes on long after we have met the Lord.

I met a student whose mom, for most of her teenage life up until now, had been ill in such a way that she didn't know

In the end, there
will be no room to
underestimate what
God was doing when
it seemed he was
doing nothing.

when the last goodbye to her mom would be. Last semester, her mom passed away. Last Christmas was the first one her family celebrated without her mom. At one point, someone from her parish asked, "Isn't it hard to not have your mom here at Christmas?" And she also said, "Isn't it so sad that your mom won't get a chance to hold your nephew, her grandson?" First of all, these were rude remarks! Why would she ask such questions? But the student answered her like this: "Actually, my mom is still alive with Christ Jesus. My mom knows my nephew. She is alive in Christ, and her life is not over. Her chapter on this earth is finished, but her life is not over. I'm not about to stay in darkness." The love of God that was true in the light is still true in the darkness.

The *Catechism* sums up the hope we have, even when we find ourselves walking in darkness. In the end, it says, "We shall know the ultimate meaning of the whole work of creation." In the end, we will "understand the marvelous ways by which [God's] Providence led everything towards its final end." In the end, "The Last Judgment will reveal that God's justice triumphs over all the injustices committed by his creatures and that God's love is stronger than death" (1040). In the end, we realize that our brokenness was not only helpful; it was necessary. We needed that brokenness. And that hiddenness wasn't just helpful; we needed it. And we needed to walk in darkness. In the end, there will be no room to underestimate what God was doing when it seemed he was doing nothing.

May we never underestimate what God is doing when it seems he is doing nothing.

JUST SHOW UP

How to Handle the Unimpressive Seasons of Life

Who is the most important, influential person in your life? Maybe one of your parents or your spouse or a close friend? It could be your supervisor at work or an aunt or uncle who was deeply invested in your upbringing. My guess is that if you were to step back and put aside the impact that person made on your life, you'd probably conclude they were pretty ordinary. You would look at their day-to-day lives and see that they were filled with everyday tasks: grocery shopping, working at their job, picking up their kids, maybe volunteering at their parish. They weren't superheroes or great movers and shakers in the world. They were just ordinary people.

In this chapter, I want to look at what growth in the Lord really looks like. I think when it comes to growth—when it comes to becoming the person God needs us to be—we tend to think of the breakthrough moments. We tend to think of the heroic

We cannot underestimate the importance of unimpressive moments or even seasons when it comes to becoming the people God needs us to be.

moments. Maybe it's like the athlete who in the last seconds of the game does something amazing to bring his team to victory. Or it's like the moment when your favorite singer wins on *American Idol.*

We love the peak moments. We live for those moments. But it turns out, not only are those peak moments incredibly rare; they are not nearly as important as we think they are.

Take the Long View

Two brothers, Dan and Chip Heath, have written many books. One of them is called *The Power of Moments.* They wrote about this: imagine that you took a vacation to Walt Disney World. Now, in the course of that vacation, imagine being asked at different moments to rate your vacation on a scale of one to ten. Your answers would likely be all over the board. At one moment, you'd say, "It's a ten! We just rode Space Mountain!" But at another moment, you might say, "It's a two. We've been in line for the new Star Wars ride for four hours, and we're hot and hungry." But when you're back in your air-conditioned hotel room and you just took a nap, you might give it an eight.

Then at the end of the vacation, you look back at all those ups and downs, and you would probably give it an eight or nine. Even though the vacation was made up of moments that were ones and twos and some eights and nines, you would look back and say it wasn't just this moment or that moment; it was the whole vacation that was the most important thing.

The point is that we cannot underestimate the importance of unimpressive moments or even seasons when it comes to

If we waste those seasons waiting for another peak, not only will we miss out on most of life, but I'm willing to bet that we won't even be able to recognize the peaks when they come.

becoming the people God needs us to be. It's not the massive transitions, like your first week away at college or your first job or your first kiss. It's not that birth or wedding or perfect vacation, not even that one retreat you've been looking forward to. It's just life. Just unimpressive, normal, ordinary life: the errands, the tasks, the people, the seasons, the process. Most of life is made up of unimpressive seasons. If we waste those seasons waiting for another peak, not only will we miss out on most of life, but I'm willing to bet that we won't even be able to recognize the peaks when they come.

How much of life is wasted just because we underestimate the importance of unimpressive seasons while we're waiting for life to happen? This is life! We can't always wait for the peak or for our growth to be done.

Just Show Up . . .

Let's look at the story of the Presentation of the Lord to see the difference between peak moments and everyday life (Luke 2:22-38). This story tells us about two people's "peak moments." First there's Simeon, an old man waiting for God to fulfill his promise that he would see the Messiah before he died. St. Luke tells us about the day that promise comes to pass. This is it! This is the best day of his life! Then there's Anna, who is eighty-four years old. This is the best day of her entire life as well.

How does Luke describe Anna's life? She started out with a lot of promise. She married, and she lived with her husband for seven years before he died. So Anna spent decades as a widow. What did she do during all this time? She lived an unimpressive

God wants us actively
engaged in living, not
just going through
the motions.

life. She was in the Temple night and day. She found God's presence and just stayed there fasting and praying. If you were to see Anna, you would probably not be impressed. But day after day, Anna showed up at the Temple to pray. She didn't wait around for the peak moment; she just kept showing up where she needed to be.

This is what we need to do. We need to be like Anna and just show up. This is the key: not waiting around for the peak moment, but simply showing up. Ask yourself today: Where does God need me to be? In this unimpressive season that you are probably in, where do you need to show up? Where do you need to be? We can't underestimate the unimpressive seasons. We have to show up to them.

. . . And Be Present

But it's not enough just to show up; we need to be present as well. We spend so much of our lives being present but wanting to be somewhere else. We know what it's like to show up but wish we were somewhere else. Maybe we feel that way sometimes at Mass or in prayer or maybe at some family dinners. But what if we not only showed up but became actively engaged, no matter where we were? What if we didn't just go through the motions but actually believed and trusted that we were where God wanted us to be? God wants us actively engaged in living, not just going through the motions. He wants us believing and trusting that he is here, and that he wants us here too.

Simeon's story reminds me of Blessed Solanus Casey, who died in 1957. When he was young, he discerned a vocation to

If we spend all our time underestimating the unimpressive seasons, we'll miss out on being the people God needs us to be.

the priesthood and joined the Capuchin order. But Solanus wasn't very successful in his seminary studies. In the end, he was ordained as a "simplex priest." He was allowed to celebrate Mass, but he wasn't allowed to preach in public or hear confessions. What was his job? Answering the door. That was his job for the rest of his life, in every friary where he lived. He sat at the front door and waited for people to come and visit the other friars.

That season of his life was absolutely unimpressive, and that season of his life made him a remarkable human being. He believed this truth: *God is here, and God wants me here.* To show up and actually be present means, like Simeon, to show up and say, *God is here, and God wants me here. He's involved in this, and I cannot underestimate this unimpressive season.*

Solanus also led a weekly prayer service and helped in the formation of a soup kitchen in downtown Detroit, but he spent most of his time simply welcoming visitors. That season of Solanus' life was unimpressive, but it made him a remarkable human being because he didn't just show up; he was present. He believed that God wanted him there, and so he stayed there.

Whenever someone would come to the door of the friary, Solanus saw that person as having been brought there by God. And as a result of his just being present, Solanus had an effect on countless people. Hundreds of people attributed miraculous healings to Solanus' prayer for them. Troubled, anxious people found peace through his words. Just because he showed up and was present.

This is what I mean when I say that if we spend all our time underestimating the unimpressive seasons, not only will we miss out on life, but we'll also miss out on being the people God needs us to be.

When life gets confusing,
just do what you know.
Just start with the
Ten Commandments.

This is also true when it comes to prayer. Our relationship with God is prayer. So much of prayer is just showing up and being there. Just show up, knowing that God is here, and God wants me here. It's really easy to do that and be frustrated. To show up, try to focus, and to think that nothing is happening, that there is no growth. But in the peak moment of Simeon's life, Simeon saw the Messiah.

Do What You Know

There are two other characters in the story of the Presentation: Mary and Joseph. Put yourself in their shoes. Here they have this baby, the Son of God, and they must have been wondering, "What do we do next?" Imagine them in those days after Jesus was born, going back to Nazareth—with God in their arms—wondering what came next. They did what they knew. And they knew that the Law of Moses said that on the fortieth day, they should bring their child to the Temple for the rite of purification. So that's what they did. They followed the commands of God.

We can make life so confusing at times, but the answer is often very simple: when life gets confusing, just do what you know. Just start with the Ten Commandments. If you're attracted to someone who is already married and you don't know what to do, it's simple: the ninth commandment says you shouldn't do anything. Or if you really want something but you don't own it and you want to take it, the sixth commandment tells you not to take it. It's that simple. You show up, you make sure you're present, and you do what you know. Just like Mary and Joseph. Even in those unimpressive seasons of life.

Maybe all of these unimpressive seasons are only preparing you for *that* moment—the moment when you stand before God.

Suddenly

So don't underestimate the unimpressive seasons! Trust that God wants you to be where you are. Because the unimpressive seasons serve a real purpose: they get you ready. Think about the words from the prophet Malachi: "I am sending my messenger —/ he will prepare the way before me; / And the lord whom you seek will come suddenly to his temple" (3:1). You're going to get ready, you're going to prepare, and then suddenly something is going to happen. And you're going to be prepared. The question is: prepared for what? The unimpressive seasons get you ready for that moment when something suddenly happens.

But what is this sudden thing that will happen? It may not be something impressive that gets you noticed or makes you famous or important. Maybe all of these unimpressive seasons are only preparing you for *that* moment—the moment when you stand before God. Maybe they're preparing you for that moment when suddenly all of the unimpressive seasons that seemed so unimportant and underestimated make sense. Maybe it's all for that moment when you will be who God needs you to be. At that moment, you'll see what he's been doing. And in that moment, because you refused to underestimate the importance of the unimpressive seasons, in that greatest moment of your life, at the peak moment of your life, you'll be ready to see him.

REFLECTION and DISCUSSION

I believe that many of us have underestimated our role in God's story, and because of that, we have underestimated who God needs us to be.

Are there any ways in which you might be underestimating your role in God's story? If so, how might a new outlook on your role affect your ability to be who he needs you to be?

Saints are just people who didn't underestimate who God needed them to be.

Think about a saint that you admire. Maybe it's your Confirmation saint or someone whose qualities you appreciate. What is it that you admire about them? Is it what they were able to accomplish in their lifetime? Or perhaps the love they were able to show to people so undeserving of their love? As you think about this person, consider that their holiness and ability to follow God hinged on their "yes" to God's full plan for them. How can you imitate them and give God your full "yes" today?

What would a 1 percent change look like in your life?

If your single unifying principle is to know Jesus, what can you do to know him better? What could help you to stick with this 1 percent change in your life?

If becoming who God needs us to be is the project of our lives, we have to be prepared to actually let it take our entire lives.

How does this statement affect your understanding of what it means to walk with God? At the same time, how can you care for yourself and others today in order to continue being who God needs you to be in the future?

God's silence is not the same thing as his absence.

Have you ever felt like God wasn't hearing or answering your prayers? As Fr. Mike recounts, from the moment Daniel started to pray, God heard him, but Daniel didn't know that. Does the story of Daniel encourage you to think about your unanswered prayers differently?

To live in this world of uncertainty is to walk in darkness.

How has time given you perspective on past seasons in your life that were confusing or difficult? How does remembering those seasons help you trust in God's goodness and faithfulness today? What are some ways that you can keep going, even when you feel like you're in darkness?

We cannot underestimate the importance of unimpressive moments or even seasons when it comes to becoming the people God needs us to be.

Are there any "peak moments" that you are driven by? How has this been helpful to you? In what ways has it been unhelpful? Fr. Mike reminds us that these moments are rare and much of life is made up of "unimpressive" moments or seasons. Think about some unimpressive seasons in your life. How do you believe God was shaping you to be who he needs you to be?

Ask yourself today: Where does God need me to be? In this unimpressive season that you are probably in, where do you need to show up?

In reading through this booklet and the insights that Fr. Mike shares, consider the following questions: Where do you sense that God is asking you to be more present? And where is he asking you to be less involved?

Maybe all of these unimpressive seasons are only preparing you for *that* moment—the moment when you stand before God.

Imagine the length of eternity compared to the timeline of your life on the earth. Now imagine how much of your life on the earth is made up of mundane, unimpressive moments and tasks. How are these preparing you for eternal life? How does this give you a new perspective on what might seem like an unimpressive season in your life?

About Fr. Mike Schmitz

Fr. Mike Schmitz is chaplain for the Newman Catholic Campus Ministry at the University of Minnesota-Duluth and Director of Youth and Young Adult Ministry for the Diocese of Duluth. He is also the host of *The Bible in a Year* podcast, produced by Ascension and available for free at ascensionpress.com/biy or on the Ascension App. Other popular offerings from Fr. Mike include his weekly videos on the Ascension Presents YouTube channel, his Sunday Mass videos, and his homilies podcast. To learn more, visit ascensionpress.com/fathermike.

Resources by Fr. Mike Schmitz

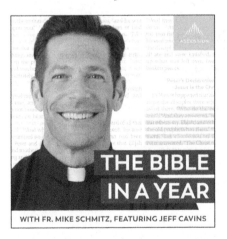

In Ascension's chart-topping *Bible in a Year* podcast, Fr. Mike Schmitz guides Catholics through the Bible in 365 daily episodes. Father Mike follows a one-of-a-kind reading plan inspired by the Great Adventure Bible Timeline® learning system, developed by renowned Catholic Bible teacher Jeff Cavins. Get started for free at ascensionpress.com/biy.

Pocket Guide to Reconciliation
By Fr. Mike Schmitz and Fr. Josh Johnson

Experience joy and freedom in the Sacrament of Reconciliation with the best-selling *Pocket Guide to the Sacrament of Reconciliation.* In this small but powerful book, Fr. Mike and Fr. Josh explain:

» How to make an excellent examination of conscience

» How to identify the root cause of sins you find yourself confessing over and over again

» What to do if you don't feel sorry for your sins

» And more!

Learn more at ascensionpress.com/reconciliation.

Come to the Altar: Worshipping God with Your Whole Heart
By Fr. Mike Schmitz

In this short booklet, Fr. Mike Schmitz teaches Catholics how to fully worship the Lord in the Holy Sacrifice of the Mass instead of just going through the motions. Learn more at ascensionpress.com/cometothealtar.

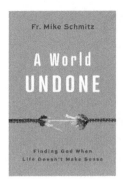

A World Undone
Finding God When Life Doesn't Make Sense
by Fr. Mike Schmitz

Product Code: BMSUE0
ISBN: 978-1-59325-599-2

Discover the one thing that changes everything! In this booklet, Fr. Mike unfolds the mystery of brokenness. He reminds us that we have been fought for by a God who wants us as we are, not as we should be or hope to be. The Lord's will for us is to find our identity in him and to thrive, living the life he has given us.
Order at bookstore.wau.org.

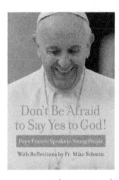

Don't Be Afraid to Say Yes to God!
Pope Francis Speaks to Young People, with Reflections by Fr. Mike Schmitz

Product Code: BPFPE8
ISBN: 978-1-59325-328-8

Set out for the future without fear! That's the message of Pope Francis to young people as he challenges them to follow Christ and his plan for their lives. In this collection of short excerpts of his talks from around the world, Pope Francis speaks to the best instincts of young people, inviting them to do their part to build a better, more just world. He encourages teens and young adults to say yes to all that God is asking of them, even while acknowledging that following the Lord wholeheartedly involves risks as well as rewards. Fr. Mike provides follow-up reflections and questions after each selection that are designed to help young people draw closer to God in prayer, giving them the courage to rise up and embrace the pope's words. This book can profoundly influence the choices that young people make at crucial decision points in their lives. Order at bookstore.wau.org.

the WORD among us®

The Word Among Us publishes a monthly devotional magazine, books, Bible studies, and pamphlets that help Catholics grow in their faith.

To learn more about who we are and what we publish, visit www.wau.org. There you will find a variety of Catholic resources that will help you grow in your faith.

Your review makes a difference! If you enjoyed this book, please consider sharing your review on Amazon using the QR code below.

Embrace His Word
Listen to God . . .

www.wau.org

Made in the USA
Coppell, TX
11 October 2024

38531373R00036